Maasai

Maasai

Photographs by Cynthia Salvadori
Text by Andrew Fedders

COLLINS

St James's Place, London, 1973

WILLIAM COLLINS SONS & CO LTD

LONDON · GLASGOW · SYDNEY · AUCKLAND

TORONTO · JOHANNESBURG

ISBN 0 00 211947 1

First published 1973
Reprinted 1978

Photographs © Cynthia Salvadori, 1973
Text © Andrew Fedders, 1973

Design by Alan Coombes

Set in Monotype Ehrhardt

Made and printed in Great Britain at
the Alden Press, Oxford

For Meja, Peter, Rocca and our other Keekonyokie Maasai friends, and their way of life

Introduction

In the restless eyes of people spawned by urban-orientated cultures, bounded by bureaucracy and bored by the lifelong drudgery of 'honest labour', a nomad roams the Elysian Fields of once-upon-a-time, happier, far away places. The romance of his existence is enhanced by its contrast to that of his neighbour in passing, the earthbound, soil-scratching cultivator; it is compounded by fact and myth and the stuff of daydreams. A nomad leads a wandering life, but his mobility is limited by water and by grazing. Though springtime pastures of plenty may flow with milk from his herds and the honey of wild bees, the fat of the land is too soon stripped to dusty bone. Star-crowded night skies are more benign than the constricting shelter of alien laws in towns, yet his traditions tyrannise and blood ties bind. Even if not entirely tied to time and place, he is still at the mercy of nature's own wayward whims. And so it goes. Fact and myth contradict, or balance, and thus cancel, one another. Daydreams exaggerate them indiscriminately. Perhaps this romantic vision of an alternative is necessary to those who feel walled in by the mass of their fellows. In an overly organised world, in which the individual is regulated, summarised and predicted on paper, it is only natural to admire those peoples – Bedouins, Tuaregs, Somalis, Maasai and their like – who manage to lead uncluttered lives in the narrowing margins of relative freedom.

This book expresses our personal admiration for one of these peoples, the pastoral and semi-nomadic Maasai.

Thousands of years ago a people called the Nilotes lived in the Nile River basin, in the southern part of present day Sudan. They were a tall and slender Negroid sub-race who spoke languages of the Eastern sub-family of the Sudanic stock and subsisted by hunting and gathering. Around 3000 BC the art of crop cultivation diffused across the continent from western Africa, and during the ensuing centuries the Nilotes began to till the soil. But they did not flourish as an agricultural people. So between the sixth and ninth centuries AD the Nilotes turned their efforts to the less arduous pursuit of stock-raising. Whether they were introduced to animal husbandry by another people, or whether they had engaged in it previously as an un-developed adjunct to agriculture, we do not know. Whichever the case, the Nilotes dis-covered their *métier*. Some, living in environ-ments favourable to agriculture, devoted them-selves to animal husbandry as well as cultivation. Others, inhabiting less suitable areas, developed stock-raising to such an extent that it no longer merely supplemented agriculture, but became the dominant factor of their economic life. These latter Nilotes became pastoral nomads. Territorial expansion was inevitable. The pastoral Nilotes migrated southward.

To the east of the Nilotes, in northeastern Africa, lived the Cushites, a group of peoples belonging to the Mediterranean sub-race of Caucasoids and speaking a Hamitic language called Cushitic. Those inhabiting the Ethiopian highlands developed a sophisticated system of agriculture based on terracing and irrigation. Because of the elaborate stonework involved, they are known as the Megalithic Cushites. They also moved southward. Why they moved is a matter of conjecture. It is a fact, however, substantiated by archeological remains, that by approximately 1000 BC the Megalithic Cushites were settling in the rainy highland areas of what is now East Africa. Their arrival displaced many of the indigenous Bushmanoid people, the little hunters and gatherers who dwelt in scattered numbers throughout much of the southern half of the continent.

In the course of their progress southward the Nilotes encountered near Lake Victoria the highly evolved states established by the Bantu peoples who had been pushing eastward from the Congo basin in preceding centuries. This Bantu barrier deflected the Nilote migration further to the east, into the lands of the Megalithic Cushites. And so, less than a millennium ago, the Nilotes engulfed the Megalithic Cushites – not through carnage, but through intermarriage, birthing the forebearers of the Maasai – and dispersed the remaining Bushmanoids from the surrounding savanna lands.

The resultant mixture eventually produced somewhat different peoples. Members of what we call the Kalenjin group, for example, became primarily agriculturalists, and groups such as the Maasai continued to be pastoralists. (There are Maasai-speaking people who raise crops, but they are of relatively recent agricultural persuasion, in minority and despised by the pastoral Maasai.) Among the Maasai the physical characteristics of the Nilotes are dominant. The language, Maa, from which their name derives, is fundamentally that of the Nilotes too, although Cushitic elements have survived. Their culture reflects the dual ancestry more equitably. Pastoralism, the absence of any centralised or complex form of political organisation and the removal of both lower incisors are Nilotic traits; the organisation of society into age-grades, the drinking of blood obtained from living animals by means of a miniature arrow shot from a bow, and the circumcision of boys and clitoridectomy of girls are Cushitic features.

A gap of several centuries follows the Nilote absorption of the Megalithic Cushites. It is a historical blank until the southward migration of the Cushitised Nilotes known as Maasai. This movement probably began prior to the seventeenth century and is recorded in a Maasai legend about 'ascending the escarpment'. They left the Kerio River Valley region of northwestern Kenya, near Lake Rudolph, and wandered down to the more abundant grazing in the Great Rift Valley and on the surrounding plains. When the first European explorers trudged across East Africa the Maasai were already ensconced in their new lands.

These new lands knew no bounds and ranged as widely as the Maasai roamed. And they roamed from the deserts north of Mount Kenya to the plains south of Mount Kilimanjaro, and from the shores of Lake Victoria to the beaches of the Indian Ocean, as if this vast expanse were their private domain. A band of young warriors would raid one place one day and be fifty, sixty miles away the next, surprising somebody somewhere else. They were ubiquitous. They were the constant scourge of other tribes. Or were they? Recall the parenthetically mentioned Maasai-speaking people, those of agricultural persuasion. The pastoral Maasai – the true Maasai – call them *Iloikop. Iloikop* were the culprits more often than not, but most victims and witnesses did not or could not distinguish between them and the purely pastoral Maasai. This lack of discernment has subjected the Maasai to an undeservedly defaming reputation. The Maasai, after all, held the *Iloikop* in check and thrice last century defeated them in major wars.

Ultimately the Maasai defeated themselves, with nature's unkind collusion. Rinderpest attacked their cattle in 1890. It devastated the herds. Drought followed rinderpest. Famine trailed in those dry and diseased tracks. Next smallpox reared its pestilential head and over half the Maasai died. In sheer desperation some sections of the tribe raided their neighbours for livestock. The neighbours retaliated, and soon intratribal warfare was doing to them what neither other tribes nor their own relations, the *Iloikop*, had been able to do. Yet the catastrophe was by no means concluded. In 1889 the influential *Laibon* (chief priest or prophet or seer or ritual expert – the meanings are manifold), Mbatian, died. His two sons disputed the succession, rival factions formed among the sections, the dissension became entangled with the raids and reprisals, and the already hopeless situation degenerated further into civil war.

The Maasai have recovered from those days of despair, those days which dragged through a decade. Numerically they prosper. Their population today is roughly 120,000 and straddles the Kenya-Tanzania border. But the memories of old men stretch far back and grip tightly. Circumstances have invaded the Maasai in the past. They may invade again in the future. There is no defence against them. There is only the comfort and consolation of custom. That is how the old men reason. The Maasai therefore remain traditionalists. Their concessions to change are grudging.

Maasai society is a man's society, structured around the age-grade functions of the male. The age-grades are four: junior warrior, senior warrior, junior elder and senior elder. The warrior age-grades constitute a fighting force in times of conflict and a corps of able men in the service of the community in times of domestic need; the elder age-grades provide an administrative body. A generation of males forms an age-set, and every age-set passes through each age-grade in succession. Consequently an age-set remains a permanent unit formed by males of the same generation, whereas an age-grade is a temporary stage in life. Every age-set consists initially of two age-groups. One group is the 'right hand circumcision', the older boys of a generation who are circumcised first. The other is the 'left hand circumcision', the younger boys of a generation who are circumcised later. Both age-groups serve as junior warriors for a period of three to seven years, but because the 'right hand' begin their warriorhood some seven years earlier than the 'left hand', and because both 'right hand' and 'left hand' conclude their warrior years at the same time, the 'right hand' serve as senior warriors for a period of twelve to fifteen years and the 'left hand' for only five to eight. During the ceremony initiating them into the junior elder age-grade the two age-groups unite. Thereafter all the members of the age-set progress together through the junior and senior elder age-grades, each of which lasts approximately fifteen years.

Maasai society is remarkably egalitarian. There is no social stratification and no system of coercive authority. A man who owns many cattle is wealthy, yet a man with fewer cattle and more sons is considered wealthier. A man who is selected a leader, a spokesman for his age-mates, has prestige, but his power is merely that of a kind of chairman who presides over meetings. Traditionally the Maasai had no chiefs or headmen. The British imposed this unfamiliar form of authority and the present governments perpetuate it. In practice, however, the Maasai carry on in the old time-proven ways. Matters affecting a settlement as a unit are settled by the elders of that settlement; those affecting a locality are discussed and resolved by the various local spokesmen sitting together with the local elders' councils; and affairs involving an entire section of the tribe are managed by an *ad hoc* council made up of spokesmen and representative elders meeting only when essential. The nearly twenty sections of the Maasai people have no established pattern of co-operation among them.

The concept of individual land ownership is alien to the Maasai. Each section is not only politically autonomous, but has its own clearly defined grazing lands also. These lands are subdivided into localities. A locality is determined by the proximity and amount of a permanent water supply. The number of people and settlements in a locality depend upon the water and grazing available. A family may live where it chooses within the limits of a locality.

Life and livelihood revolve around the cattle. According to Maasai beliefs, *Enkai*, the sky (i.e., sky god, or simply god), was once one with the earth. When earth and sky separated cattle were sent to the Maasai from and by the sky, *Enkai*. The people interpret this myth of creation quite literally. To engage in any occupation other than herding is insulting to *Enkai* and demeaning to oneself. Perhaps because cattle are associated with grass, and grass with the earth, a pastoral Maasai can never consider breaking ground for cultivation. He does not even bury his dead or dig for water. His people were chosen by *Enkai* to be the recipients of cattle and they remain herders by choice. This complete dependence on cattle permeates all aspects of Maasai existence, from the common greeting of 'I hope your cattle are well' to the ceremonial slaughter of bullocks to their everyday sustenance, milk. The slightest change can affect the entire intricate texture of such a cattle-concentric society. Small wonder then that the Maasai are reluctant to adopt 'modern ways'. They have evolved their own ways over the course of centuries, and their own ways suit them admirably.

Kedong, Kenya
August 1970 – October 1971

9

Maasailand is forty thousand square miles, three-fifths of it in Tanzania and the rest in Kenya. There is grass to sustain the livestock and livestock to sustain the people, but much of the country is as poor in grazing as it is rich in wildlife and scenery.

The people live in semi-permanent settlements called *enkang*. An *enkang* is the basic economic, social and political unit. Several families group to form an *enkang* and pasture their livestock together. Although most of the inhabitants are related through extended family ties, unrelated persons often dwell among them as well.

Livestock live there too. Each family possesses its own herd. (Resorting to the convenient statistics compiled by others, the average numbers are seventy cattle, eighty-five sheep and goats, and eighteen donkeys per family.) The individual herds are pastured as one by day. In the evening the animals are driven inside the circular thorn branch barrier which encloses the *enkang*.

They do not merely live there; they play an essential part in social affairs. Animals are exchanged in a prescribed fashion to bind personal relationships such as marriage. Animals are either principals or supporting cast on most ceremonial occasions, in roles of passive victims or active participants.

Cattle are coin of the Maasai realm. Cattle-mark is synonymous with clan, because each clan has its own distinctive markings notched in the ears and scratched on the rumps of cattle. A clan's membership extends throughout Maasailand. In theory all cattle in possession of individual members are owned jointly by the clan, and if cattle are due from a member for a fine or debt they may be collected from any of his clanmates. In practice, however, the offending member or his near relatives almost always pay the amount due.

The main purpose of livestock is, of course, to
provide the people with food. Milk is the basic
item in their diet, and cows are milked twice daily.

Both fresh milk and curdled are carried and stored in gourds. Gourds are the most prevalent of household utensils and are obtained through trade with agricultural tribes. They are decorated with beads and cowrie shells, fitted with caps which also serve as cups, and fastened to leather straps to wrap around the hand and hold when milking.

Sheep and goats are the main source of meat for
most of the people, but they eat meat infrequently
and never 'in the same stomach' (together) with
milk. Healthy cows are much too precious as milk
suppliers, good bulls as breeders and bullocks as
ceremonial meat. The meat of wild animals is
never eaten, except in times of famine. Even
then it is restricted to eland and buffalo, animals
which resemble cattle. Warriors consume more
meat than the others. They need not have the
excuse of a ceremony to slaughter bullocks—if
they are in good supply.

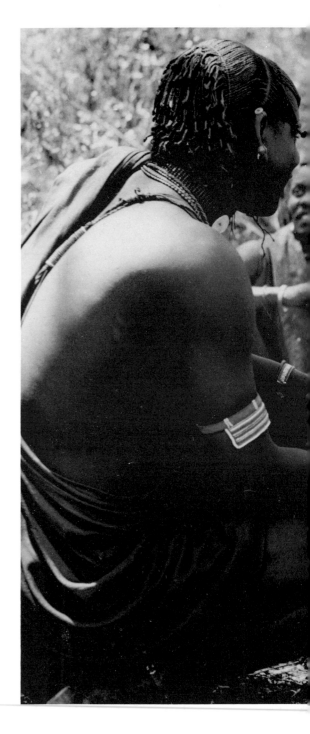

Warriors must, however, eat meat 'in the forest'
(in the bush, or out of sight), because it is
forbidden them to eat any meat which has been
seen, let alone touched, by women.

Blood is an important supplement to the basically dairy diet. A rope is drawn tightly around the neck of a bullock or cow to expose the jugular vein. A specially blocked miniature arrow is shot from close up to just pierce the wall of the vein. As the blood spurts out it is caught in a gourd. When the required amount has been tapped – and the Maasai know exactly how much the individual animal can safely give – a few hairs from the hide and a pinch of cattle dung are stuffed into the puncture. The hide around the puncture is squeezed together until the blood coagulates. The animal is then released.

The blood is stirred to remove filaments. When the filaments have been twined around a stick the blood is mixed with milk and consumed.

Food also has its ritual uses. At one stage of the *embolosat* ceremony, for example, specially selected women spray the participating boys with milk. Men would receive the same shower after a cattle raid or lion hunt.

When not actually used, milk is symbolised by a mixture of white chalk and water. The chalk is fetched in gourds from secret places by men dressed in women's clothing.

The white designs distinguish a celebrant from
the crowd.

Sometimes the celebrants are the crowd.

Unblemished bullocks are the most highly valued
of sacrificial beasts. They are ritually slaughtered
and consumed at major ceremonies.

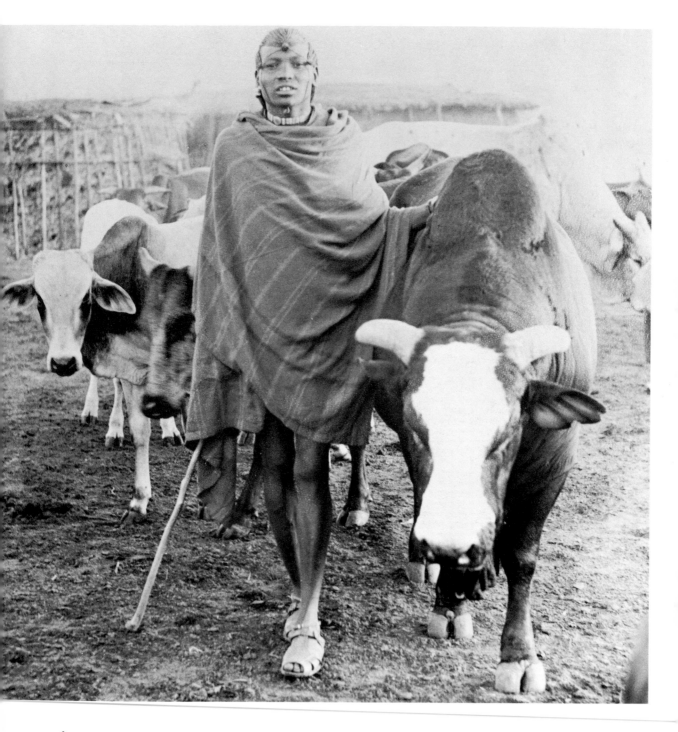

Ritual meat on the hoof or ritual meat on a stick, the flesh of animals fulfils ceremonial demands as well as feeds people.

Any animal may be ceremoniously treated, particularly if it is a favourite pet. A carved ivory amulet distinguishes its presence in a herd.

The ivory is a treasured find, perhaps a gift from god, *Enkai* (because how often does one find a piece of ivory lying on the ground?).

The chance discovery of every such item, even
one as simple as a duiker's foot, can be considered
a token of *Enkai*.

Grass too has ceremonial significance through its direct association with cattle. The Maasai believe that when *Enkai* sent them cattle he did so by means of the long aerial roots of the wild fig tree.

Therefore whenever the people pass a wild fig they honour the tree and *Enkai* by placing a handful of grass among the roots.

During some ceremonies, such as circumcision, a main participant, such as the father, carries a gourd stoppered with grass.

Cowrie shells symbolise fertility and their
decorative presence is pervasive, from milk
gourds to warrior hairdos.

The earth grows grass which feeds the livestock, who give milk and blood and meat to feed the people. It is fertile. A Maasai woman who is not fertile will attempt to stimulate pregnancy by sculpturing a little earthen doll to show *Enkai* that she wants a child.

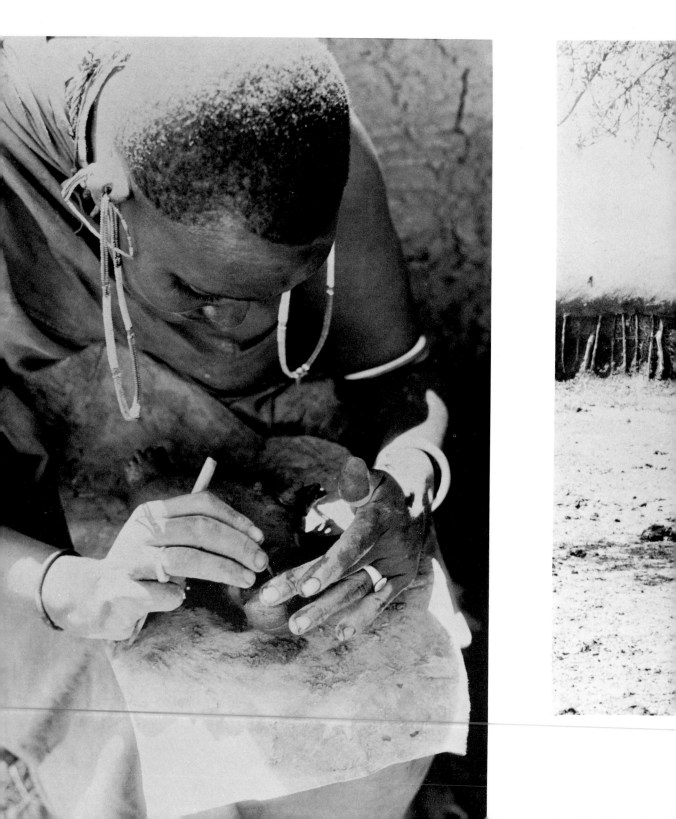

When a baby is due, women of the *enkang* and female friends and relations from the neighbourhood come to call on the expectant mother.

The birth must take place in the expectant mother's hut; it is considered bad luck for the baby to be born elsewhere.

After the baby is safely born, under the super-
vision of a midwife, the visiting women slaughter
a sheep. The baby is given a temporary pet name,
because the first months of its life are precarious.
The baby's hair is allowed to grow. It will be subjected to its first haircut the day that it receives
its proper name.

The child may continue to suckle until the age of two or more. But weaning is no problem; attention is easily diverted from breast to gourd.

The mother does not resume sexual relations with her husband until her child is weaned.

Increasing mobility carries the child closer to
responsibility. First chores may resemble games,
but first toys are everyday household things.

As the child grows, responsibilities grow, and so does respect for elders. Shaking, or rather touching, hands is the customary greeting between equals, but a young person must approach elders, and therefore betters, with an inclined head.

A young girl helps her mother with housework, carrying water, gathering wood and looking after the baby, who depends as much on its sister as on the neck and ankle amulets worn for good luck until weaning. The relationships between children are affection-filled. Older children are invariably conscientious in their baby-sitting duties – in spite of provocations.

A self-conscious sophistication develops during
the approach of physical maturity.

A girl, *ndito*, becomes a companion to a junior warrior in the locality's warrior camp. Pregnancy is not a common occurrence since the *ndito* has not yet attained puberty. If, however, an *ndito* does become pregnant, her alternatives are two: abortion by means of herbs, or the soonest possible clitoridectomy to enable her to marry. A man will automatically adopt any child born to his wife prior to their marriage, because physical paternity is of minimal importance to the Maasai.

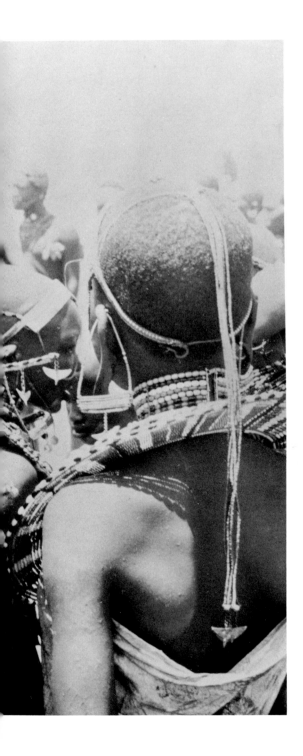

Normally an *ndito* undergoes clitoridectomy when she attains puberty. Her parents notify friends and relations of the coming ceremony and the guests come bearing gifts of milk and livestock for the feast. At dawn of the chosen day the *ndito* is seated on a cattlehide and held firmly in place by a few of the participating women while the operation is performed. During the healing interval the *ndito* is considered 'unclean'. This state is symbolised by her not being permitted to wash. Neither is she allowed to leave the vicinity of her *enkang*, nor to speak to any male not of her family. She wears a special headband which identifies her as *enkaibartani* 'one who awaits healing'. With healing comes the ritual head-shave and the beginning of womanhood.

The very young woman, still in her early teens, is now suitable for marriage. In spite of her youth it is not uncommon for the husband to be considerably older if she is to be a second, third or yet greater numbered wife. Arrangements are conducted through the parents. Initial arrangements are made and gifts presented before the clitoridectomy. Traditional gifts include three heifers, a bullock, honey, blankets, tobacco and beer. When the *enkaibartani* interval ends, the young woman's father advises the groom that his bride is ready and that he should bring the remainder of the gifts. The groom then goes to collect his bride with two rams and a ewe in tow, the latter a present for the mother. Dancing and singing by friends and relations is part of womanhood's first festive event.

Parting from the family is more solemn. Mother and grandmother burden the bride with last minute advice as thoroughly as they have burdened the donkeys with her baggage. She is off to her husband's *enkang*, where he will establish her in a house of her own and entrust her with a herd of cattle.

A woman is literally a homemaker, because
building a house is woman's work. Leafy
branches of *leleshwa*, a bush which termites find
unappetising, are woven into a crisscross frame-
work of *leleshwa* stems, and the whole is plastered
with a water-proof coating of cattle dung.

The house is her domain. It is partitioned into three rooms. Just inside the snail-shell-like entryway is a long and narrow room, the length of the house, used for stabling calves and kids and lambs at night. The passage skirts this enclosure and leads into the combination living, sleeping, cooking and eating area. At the far end of this main room is a slightly elevated platform, constructed of poles and covered with cowhide. During the day it serves for seating family and visitors, and at night it functions as a communal bed for husband (if he has only one wife, he sleeps there regularly; if more than one, he divides his periods of residence equally among the wives' houses), family and visiting relatives or friends. Facing the main room is the wife's private room. Like the stabling enclosure it is walled off from the main room by stripped and tied *leleshwa* stems. Inside is a small bed on which the woman and her smallest children sleep. There also are stored her personal treasures, household and kitchen utensils, and supplies of milk and honey beer. In front of her doorway is the home fire. It cooks and heats, but does not shed much light. If more light is needed a hole is punched through the wall.

Dawn is the time of first milking. It is the woman's exclusive responsibility. Calves are brought from the house and held close to the cows to make the milk flow more readily. When a sufficient amount of milk has been drawn for the family, the calves are released to have their own breakfast. During the day cows and calves are pastured separately. In the evening the woman milks again.

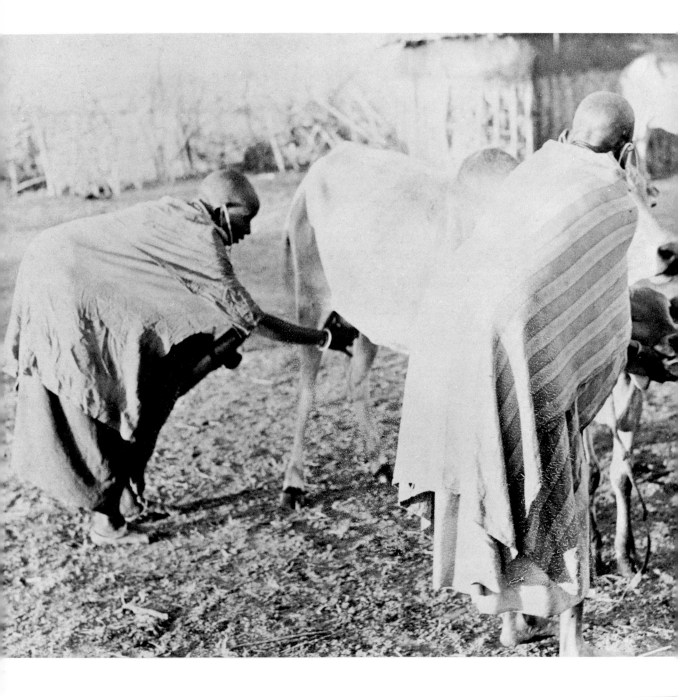

Her care encompasses kids and lambs, assisting children in that chore.

She is a sometime butcher for children and elders (no woman must touch or even see the meat which the warriors eat), but a habitual tanner and tailor for all. A hide is pegged out and carefully scraped. Then bark and animal dung are employed in the tanning. Any hide intended to be tailored for clothing is laboriously kneaded supple by hand.

Personal and household possessions are few, but made much of in every possible decorative way. A woman's bag contains her wealth of beads and ornaments.

During the rains, when most of the inhabitants of an *enkang* disperse with their herds, a woman packs up the pieces of her household to re-assemble them temporarily somewhere else. If water or grazing give out completely, she and the *enkang* make a permanent move.

A woman shoulders an impressive share of bundles herself. Firewood and water are the heaviest.

Babies are the commonest, becoming almost perpetual appendages.

Housework, childbearing and childraising are among the inevitable bonds of marriage, but there are obvious benefits to this state. A woman acquires a special elegance through marriage. Only a married woman adorns her poise with the long sheepskin skirt rainbowed by a thousand beads. The skirt is sewn from the four skins included in the bridegroom's gifts. An iron ankle-ring, yet another gift from the bridegroom, is placed by him around her ankle on their wedding day.

Wide, flat leather earrings are also inserted on that day, a day which every Maasai woman eventually celebrates. There are no spinsters among them. After marriage a woman is supposed to be available to any member of her husband's circumcision group except those of the same clan as herself. This tradition does not, however, oblige her to accommodate all – or any – of her husband's age-mates. The choice is entirely hers.

A woman has her head shaved regularly, setting off the elaborate array of beaded jewellery to undisputed advantage. She in turn shaves her friends' heads and those of her husband and children. Headshaving is not only traditional grooming, but part of every *rite de passage* as well. Birth, christening, circumcision, marriage, progression through the age-grades – each is marked by a ritual shave, using a ritual mixture of milk and water.

Beads and coils of wire were brought to the Maasai in trade and as gifts for generations. The Arabs introduced Venetian glass beads and the early explorers followed their example, trading for essential foods and paying for the right of passage. Although the metal and beads still come from without Maasailand, design and workmanship are uniquely Maasai.

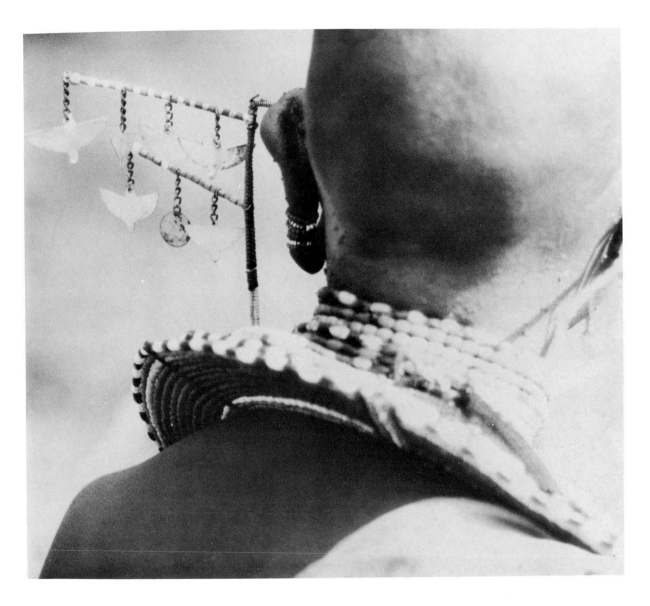

Coils of wire form a decorative load in which a married woman may sheathe her legs. (An apocryphal 'legend' that a Maasai told us has it that this added weight made it difficult, if not impossible, for a raiding enemy to drive or carry off a much prized wife. On another occasion a Maasai woman laughingly described them as 'soksi wa Maasai tu' – only Maasai stockings.)

Coils of wire on the upper arm have a definite meaning. They show that a child has been circumcised.

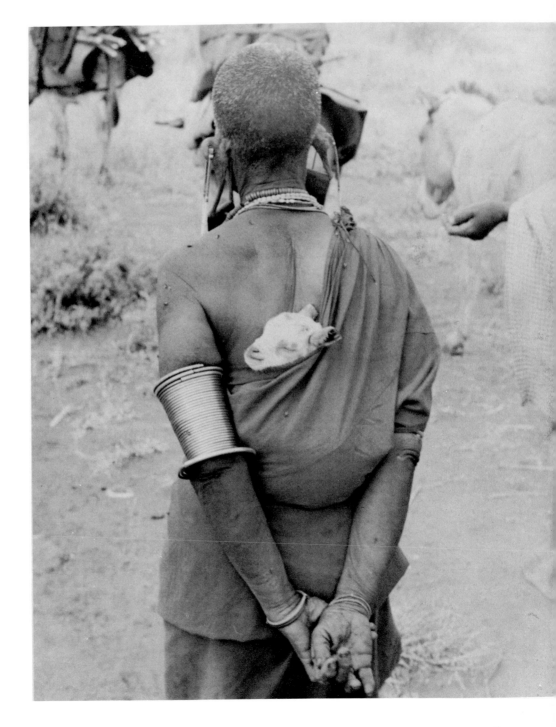

As her sons are circumcised and become warriors, a woman comes under their nominal guardianship. When the sons leave the *enkang* for their own encampment the mother may accompany them. If the mother accompanies them, she takes along the cattle which were allocated to her when she became a wife. When the sons marry and decide to live in an *enkang* other than their father's, the mother may move with them again, but only if her husband has other, younger wives to look after him and his cattle.

A woman is not alone in her old age. The youngest son looks after her until she dies. Meanwhile her responsibilities are few and there is ample opportunity to sit and watch the *enkang*'s daily life until her own ends.

Little girls pattern themselves after their mothers and sisters. Little boys posture themselves after their fathers and brothers. Both learn through imitation and early achieve proficiency in comportment and chores.

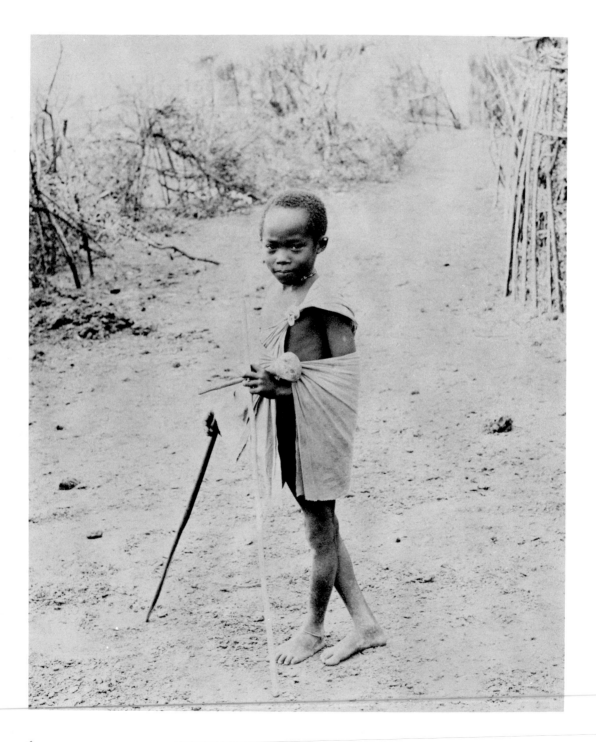

A boy is the family herder. At the age of four or five, when his lower incisors are removed, he is entrusted with lambs, kids and very young calves. Between the ages of five and seven, when the tops of his ears are pierced, he becomes responsible for slightly older animals and may accompany elders herding cattle. When the boy is considered capable of looking after fully grown animals and of herding them from pasture to pasture, his lobes are pierced.

Transformation from boyhood to warriorhood – and full membership in the tribe – is accomplished through a series of ceremonies, the most crucial of which is circumcision. The ceremony which officially opens the circumcision period for all Maasailand is called the *embolosat*. It is performed roughly once every fifteen years by the Keekonyokie section, with guests from neighbouring sections in attendance, and affects every Maasai boy who has achieved physical maturity or is approaching puberty. For the participating boy the climax of the ceremony occurs when a bull is set loose by the sponsoring elders and he, together with the other boys, runs off in pursuit. The object of the chase is literally to grab the bull by his horns and throw him to the ground. The boy who grabs the right horn gains distinction among his age-mates.

Already during these pre-circumcision ceremonies age-group leaders are selected and social
responsibilities begin. Mental maturity is the
criterion for a 'chief councillor'. For the ceremonial leadership of the *embolosat*, and thus
subsequent influence in the age-group, a
family's reputation influences the choice. The
boy who is picked provides the bull to be chased,
wrestled and slaughtered.

A recruiting campaign follows the *embolosat*. A boy ready for circumcision bands together with other boys to roam the countryside collecting more boys to form the locality's 'right hand circumcision' (in approximately seven years the younger boys of the generation will do the same to form the 'left hand circumcision'). When all suitable candidates have been gathered, the group retires to a secluded spot in the company of their sponsors, the junior elders. A bullock is slaughtered, blessings are invoked and strips of the bullock's hide are given to each boy as a sign that he is a member of the circumcision group. The boy then wears these strips of hide as bracelets.

As the time for the actual operation approaches the boy begins to hunt small birds. He is not allowed to trap them, but must knock them out of trees by throwing clubs. The birds killed are skinned and the skins are stuffed with straight stiff stems of dry grass. Their feathers are smoothed and polished with a piece of sheepskin. Lastly the conical figures are fitted into a wooden frame to form a headdress which the boy will wear after his circumcision.

Saplings signal from the rooftop that a newly circumcised son lies within. The young man recuperates from the operation in the privacy of his mother's room.

In a week or so the *olaibartani* is up and about. He is easily identified by the coiled metal earrings fixed to the sides of his head. The earrings belong to his mother and are loaned to him for the healing interval.

On his feet the *olaibartani* wears cowhide sandals made especially for him by one of his mother's brothers on the day before the operation. When he puts the sandals on for the first time, the *olaibartani* puts them on the wrong way around: right on left and left on right. This act safeguards him against evil spells.

A bow and wax-tipped arrows may be carried to shoot at *nditos* found outside the *enkang*. Any girl hit by one of the arrows must give a small ornament to the *olaibartani* who shot her.

A cowrie belt girds his waist and prohibitions hem his behaviour. The *olaibartani* must enter his *enkang* before the cattle do at dusk. He must neither drink blood nor touch meat with his hands (meat is cut up for him and served on a stick). Since he is considered 'unclean', sexual relations are forbidden.

In some circumstances a boy may be circumcised before he attains physical maturity. For instance, when a man dies suddenly, without having the opportunity to make bequests to all his sons, all his property passes to the eldest. The eldest son, however, must be circumcised to inherit. If the boy is very young the property is held in trust for him by his paternal uncles. He is circumcised as soon as possible and assumes the responsibilities of an elder immediately. Circumcision may therefore be regarded as recognition of a boy's mental maturity rather than merely a ritual marking the arrival of puberty.

Finally the months of being *olaibartani* end. Head and eyebrows are shaved by the mother; the bird headdress is thrown among the cattle to be trampled into dust, except for one bird which the mother saves to wear at her waist for the next four days; the cowries from the belt are given to the mother and she adorns her gourds with them; and the coiled metal earrings are returned to her also. All boyhood things are discarded. The boy has become a young man. He is *olmurrani*, or more commonly *moran*, a junior warrior.

The new *moran* joins the other new *moran* of his locality to form a company of junior warriors. They live together in an encampment called *Imanyat*, or *manyatta*, constructed for them by women. (If there are two or three adjacent localities which do not have an adequate number of *moran* to form their individual companies, the *moran* of these localities unite to a form a single company and live in a single *manyatta*.) The *manyatta* is a vast establishment. Numbers of *moran* vary between dozens and hundreds. Mothers and *nditos* may live there as well.

A *moran*'s duty is to defend the people and livestock of his locality. It is also his duty to help with the herding during the extremely dry seasons and periods of drought. His more vigorous activities have been curtailed, first by the *Pax Britannica* and then *Uhuru*. Raiding for cattle was the most popular sport. A major raid was organised and blessed by the elders, and the raiders carried a protective charm from the *laibon*. The more frequent minor raids were less formal. When he was not warring or raiding or hunting a lion, the *moran* feasted on bullocks, sang and danced, and enjoyed the company of admiring *nditos*, as he still does today.

The spear is a *moran*'s prized possession. Spears are made by the Kunono, a clan of smiths, and bought by the Maasai for the price of a calf. The thin-shafted, leaf-bladed spears are used for throwing, and the narrow-bladed ones for stabbing. The most important is the war spear, which has a very long narrow blade. Colour of the shaft is important too, black being more prestigious – and the prerogative of senior *moran* – than light.

Short swords, which cost a goat, are also made by
Ilkunono (and more recently in Birmingham).
The red leather sheaths are the work of the
WaNderobo tribe.

As many as six wooden clubs were carried into battle. Some of them were thrown at the enemy before the *moran* engaged in close combat.

A shield rounds out the arsenal. The big, sturdy
battle shield, made from buffalo hide (and
occasionally from giraffe or zebra hides), is a
beautiful oval armour and a source of pride to its
bearer. Designs on one half of the shield show the
moran's section and those on the other half his
age-group. A distinctive circular mark may be
added by fellow *moran* in the owner's absence to
proclaim his bravery.

An ostrich feather headdress was common plumage for wars, cattle raids and lion hunts. It gave a psychological advantage to the wearer by creating an illusion of vastly superior height in the eyes of the enemy. (The lion mane headdress has become somewhat of a rarity; lion hunting is restricted by law. Trophies from a hunt belong to two men: the one who grabs the lion by the tail and the one who spears the lion first.)

A *moran* still rallies to the Kudu horn's drone,
but now to ceremonies rather than battle.

The jingling din of thighbells once signalled the intimidating approach of the *moran* to their enemies. Today a *moran* dons the thighbell to dance and celebrate, producing the sound by quivering tension as well as by deliberate movement.

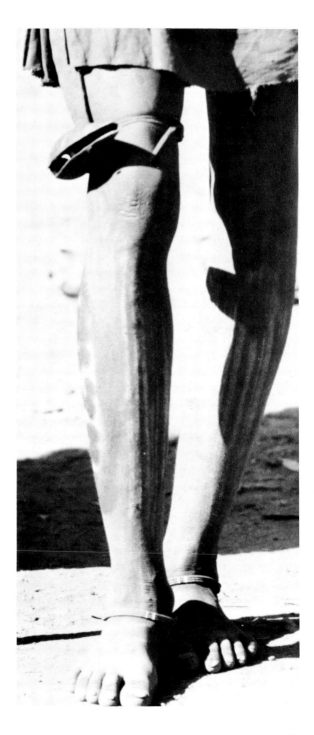

Long hair is a helmet. When a *moran*'s hair has grown to a workable thatch, a friend becomes a hairdresser for the duration of several days. First the hair is parted across the head from ear to ear. All of it is coated with a mixture of ochre (red earth) and animal fat. Next strands of hair are rubbed between fingers and palms to form miniature twisted ropes. These twisted hair ropes in front of the parting are separated into three sections – one over the forehead and one over each temple. They are then tied at the end.

The twisted hair ropes in back of the parting are gathered into a pigtail at the bottom by binding them around a carved piece of wood.

Patterns of cicatrisation trickle from the shoulders down the chest and stomach. The scarring is an optional decoration, but, if desired, must be done prior to circumcision.

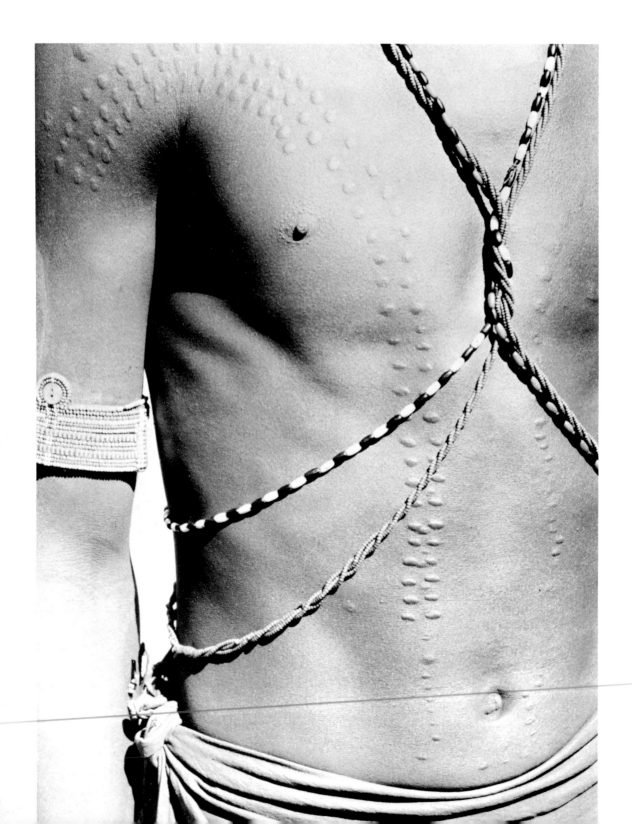

Before manufactured cloth became readily and inexpensively available, a *moran* wore a goatskin or calfskin cape as his everyday uniform. Today the common covering is a brightly coloured cloth of red or reddish orange, shades which the Maasai fancy so much. The cloth may be draped toga-fashion over one shoulder, wrapped around the body from chest to knees, suspended from criss-crossing beaded braces or rolled down around the waist loincloth style.

A cow's stomach serves as a hairnet, raincap or
covering over which to fit a headdress.

When a *moran* went on a major raid he was given two pairs of cowhide sandals. If one pair wore out or came apart, a second conveyed him quickly on his way.

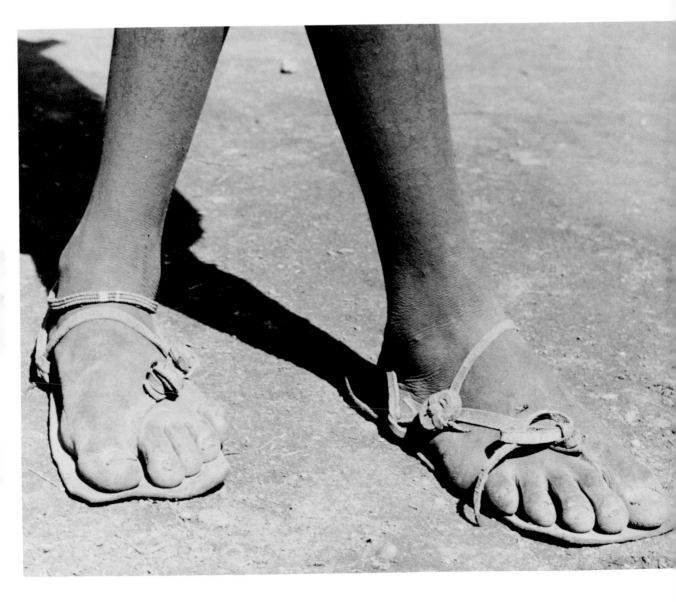

and bandoliers of beads festoon a *moran. Leleshwa*
leaves carried under the arm are not a decoration,
but a deodorant.

Bodies shine, sleek and red, smeared with ochre and animal fat. All Maasai use this mixture as a basic cosmetic, but a *moran* uses it more elaborately. Slender snakes of paint wriggle down the legs, dressing him in hip-high stockings. The ingredients are practical also: the fat provides insulation against heat and cold, and the ochre, when applied with water, removes the fat and body dirt through absorption.

For painting belongings rather than bodies, three traditionally favoured colours are used: black, made from the charcoal of burnt calabash mixed with blood from a bullock; red, made from powdered ochre mixed with blood from a bullock; and white, made from the ash of bullock bone mixed with water.

Song and dance pass time pleasantly and keep a *moran* fit.

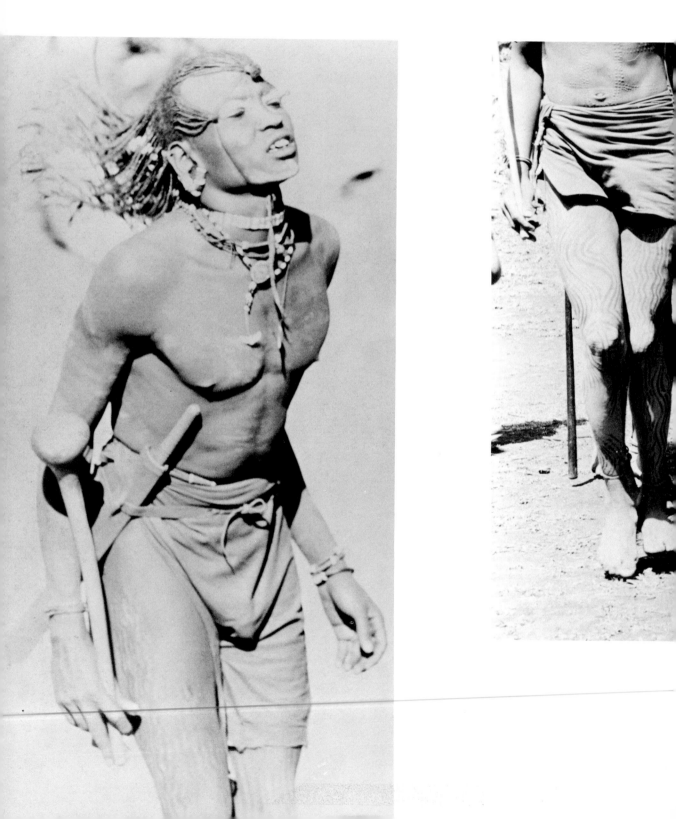

Dancing is physical exercise done to vocal rhythm.

Another diversion are the *nditos*.

The junior *moran* age-grade and life in a *manyatta* – the former three to seven years and the latter two to three – foster a sense of community, comradeship and mutual loyalty. Participation in almost every aspect of life is communal. A *moran* may neither eat nor drink alone. He may not even relieve himself in solitude. The obvious practical reason for such traditions is to prevent a single *moran* from being surprised by an enemy. But the do's and don't's of a *moran*'s life accentuate disinterested sharing also. For instance, *a moran* may not drink the milk obtained from the cattle of his own family; he must give it to his fellow *moran*, and in turn drink theirs.

After a few years the novelty and excitement of being a junior *moran* begin to diminish. The ensuing discontent leads to agitation for the privileges accorded to senior *moran*, including the right to hold dances, other than informal ones, without the permission of elders, the right to bear black-shafted spears and the right to marry. When the pressure reaches a critical point the elders agree to promotion, because it is an expedient means of eliminating a threat to authority. The ceremony celebrating promotion is called *eunoto*. The crucial rites extend over a period of four days. A new age-group leader, the *Olotuno*, judged to be a morally and physically superior youth, is selected. It is his duty to open the way in all affairs pertaining to the age-group. A ceremonial house, round and with a conical roof (totally unlike the typical Maasai dwellings), is constructed. The main events revolve around this structure.

A junior *moran* taking part in the *eunoto* sits on the same cowhide on which he was circumcised while his mother shaves his head using a moistening mixture of milk and water. If the mother has contravened any basic rules governing a woman's behaviour, a close relation takes her place (whereas if her son has contravened any basic rules governing a warrior's behaviour, he will still be shaved and promoted, but he will never become one of the elect or select, nor will he ever have the status of his well-behaved fellows). The *Olotuno* is the first to lose his hair. The others in the age-group then lose theirs. The freshly shaven head is rubbed with a mixture of red ochre and animal fat. A senior *moran* is allowed to grow his hair long again, however, and to marry – after the *Olotuno* does.

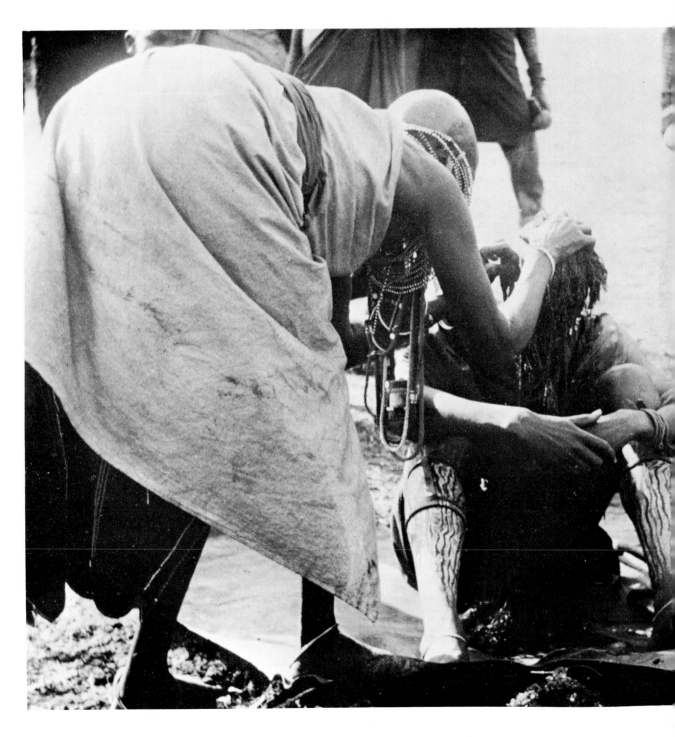

A fire is kindled on the back of a bull (a ceremonial gesture, not an infliction of pain). A bullock is slaughtered, its flesh roasted and shared by a number of young men representing the age-group. These select few, probably as many as forty-nine, do this on behalf of the entire age-group. The other members hold their own, less formal, feasts. When the ceremony ends a new age-grade begins, and the entire age-group acquires a lasting name.

More, minor, ceremonies follow. One removes the prohibition on drinking milk alone (and many marriages occur soon thereafter). Another allows a senior *moran* to eat meat in the presence of women and to eat meat which has been touched by their hands. This latter ceremony again requires the mother's coiled metal earrings and entails the smearing of cow dung mixed with milk on the face.

Just as the Keekonyokie section stage the *embolosat* for all Maasai, so the Kisongo section of the Moshi, Tanzania, area arrange the *ng'esher*. At this ceremony, and in the ones repeated by other sections, the *moran* surrender their hairdos for the last time. The two age-groups, 'right hand circumcision' and 'left hand circumcision', are united in an age-set, sharing a common name. Yet another leader is chosen. Warrior years are over and elderhood begins. A new elder, a junior elder, takes outright possession of his previously held-in-trust cattle. If he is married, and if his father is still living, the junior elder moves away from the paternal *enkang*. He is now allowed to participate in discussions involving his family and locality, and assumes the duties of a 'sponsor'. (A special relationship exists between alternate grades: junior elders are responsible for the initiation ceremonies of the junior *moran* and for supervising their activities; senior elders are similarly responsible for the senior *moran*.) Discussions and duties are traditionally transacted in the shade of trees.

The next ceremony in a lifelong series of rituals is best described as the *pater familias* ceremony. It qualifies a man to perform the required rites for his children as they grow up and go through their own series of rituals. Prior to the ceremony the man must make certain that all of his and his family's affairs are in order. Then an unblemished bullock is slaughtered and roasted. Close friends of the man and his wife assist them. The highlight of the merrymaking is when man and wife engage in a mock battle with long switches.

A black wooden club modestly marks a man as an age-set leader. It is the essential symbol of delegated authority.

Senior elderhood is the last of the four active stages in a man's life. Ultimate responsibility in the affairs of the people devolves upon its members. All affairs require discussion, and every elder has the right to have his say. Few let that privilege pass them by. Those that comprise the audience nod napping, chat among themselves and sometimes even listen. Custom is their constitution and compromise the *modus vivendi*.

En'geshui, the pebble game, absorbs attention not
bestowed on affairs of state.

If a man lives to a very old age he becomes one of the *Dasati*, an ancient retired elder, and reaches the end of social responsibility. But others still remain responsible for him. Care by the community does not cease with departure from the *manyatta*; it only concludes with death.

Generations are linked by an iron bracelet,
passing from dying father to youngest son.
Elder sons obtain theirs from the smiths to forge
their own progenital links.

ACKNOWLEDGMENTS

We are indebted to Hazel Mayers for providing the opportunity for the idea of a book to materialise; to the excellent collection in the Africana Room of McMillan Library, Nairobi, for assorted sources of information; to Professor George Peter Murdock's *Africa, Its Peoples and Their Culture History* (New York, 1959), Mr Alan H. Jacobs' *The Pastoral Masai of Kenya* (an unpublished manuscript) and Mr S. S. Ole Sankan's *The Maasai* (Nairobi, 1971) for the scholarly labours upon which we principally relied; to Mr Charles Winnington-Ingram, who has known the Maasai for thirty-five years, for reading our manuscript and generously sharing his invaluable knowledge; to our friend Thelma Sanders for the kind permission to use her three photos of the *eunoto* ceremony; and above all to the Keekonyokie Maasai themselves for their endless patience and co-operation in answering our questions and in tolerating the ever-present camera – as well as us – in their midst.